CONVERSION THEORY

DARIUS SIMPSON

CONVERSION THEORY

2018

CONTENTS

For **BOBBI LYNN** *&* **AMI**,
and other black women
sharing custody of me

For **FERGUSON**
and **MIKE BROWN**

So early in my life, I had learned that if you want something, you had better make some noise.

MALCOLM X (EL-HAJJ MALIK EL-SHABAZZ)

This struggle may be a moral one; or it may be a physical one; or it may be both moral and physical; but it must be a struggle. Power concedes nothing without a demand. It never did and it never will.

FREDERICK DOUGLAS

It is our duty to fight for our freedom. It is our duty to win. We must love each other and support each other. We have nothing to lose but our chains.

ASSATA SHAKUR

CONVERSION THEORY

THIS IS NOT AN INTRO

Once upon a time a curfew incited an uprising, after another mourning shot up where an obsidian form once was. Another lesson taught by an unlicensed teacher. Another student, or brown board to post a bullet in. After another indictment slipped through a hand, another loose grip miscarriage of justice. The people, rather the dirt the people came from, had had enough. After shock goes missing, convulsions set in. The noise of the seismic scale outcry shook loose hinges, doors opened, glass ceilings melted into decorations on the concrete. Resistance rattled like a renaissance, radical repetition raging over seas. It became truly a state of emergence. Those who ain't never created nothin' couldn't concentrate. The ruckus continued for 3 years straight, no negotiations, no demands issued, just one disruption after the other, each one larger and more damaging to storefronts than the last. An Emergency Diplomacy act is implemented. The U.S. Gov't admits it will never indict itself, announces, however, that it will grant the request of every African American in exchange for no more turmoil.

SEGREGATION

"YOU CAN'T SIT WITH US!"

We raise the roof
They raise the rent
We Harlem shake
They shakedown Harlem
We invent a dance called the whip
They pretend they don't know how, anymore.
AFRICAN AMERICAN PROVERB

Let the record clearly reflect that:

They is the polos wearing collared boys
they is the judge that pass the law to his son
they inherit stolen property, protect it with everyone else's life
they destroy all the pretty to rebuild and call it theirs
they would burn the sun back if they could
they is the hand searching afros without a warrant
they is the school bus driver that made slave jokes between stops
before we knew skin came in different flavors
they is the manager that called me a monkey by the bananas,
without ever saying "monkey"
they is the lips or mouth jail that keep paroling racist inmates
they is my eighth grade English teacher
and all the synonyms for him I met later in life
they take first, ask questions when found guilty,

they innocent, they never in trial long enough
to be proven anything else
they take liberty and justice from all
they write rules to a game and don't play by 'em
they immigrant passing for pilgrim
they intruder that changed the locks after breaking and entering
they stand on soil and demand it cave
they hollow a home and make a profit from the shell
they footprint and change the history of the land
they reassign the borders
they have boundary issues
they shake everything, but never at fault
they snatch a culture by the threads
they clothe a continent in denial
they is the reader questioning where they fit on this page
they might never find the answer in these words
they is the outsider in this story.
We inventors of magic before magic knew it had a name,
we innovative enough to pull an entire language from muscle memory
we imagine a whole dictionary
we morph music into a dialect
we speak in code, bilingual in business settings
we bend to avoid breaking
we dance with the wind
we the howl in the mouth of a dark knight
we pitch black running home
we basis for understanding, hardly cited as a source
we punch lines into to jokes
we laugh to keep from dyin

we smile big to shrink in public
we the night sky and the stars that built it
we black hole and the first things to be swallowed
we tongue-kiss a typhoon
we hardly get a break for air
we breathe and it sound like a hurricane
we heart quaking a pulse
we skin draped in catastrophe
we all that and the whole bag
we chip off the old block
we shoulder shrug and shift the weather
we got the short end of the stick
but still play that mufucka like a whole drum set
we percuss as a first language
we smile for no reason
we construct joy from scratch
we color a constellation using our bare hands
we whole galaxy in our palms
we close hand into a fist, rearrange the revolution of the planets
we walk, a tree trunk with an axe to grind
we grounded by nature
we pockets that steady gettin' stole from
still we generously give our lives for this world
most times, without choice
we here, livin' anyway
a half step away from soaring.

WINGS

Spine sprouts arms and the body doesn't second-guess the mutation
back bends to the thought of extension
cords harp vocals into morning dew
fresh smell of something new brandishing, lingers all over
hands feathered in fingers spread in opposite cardinal directions
bird floats from atop a flagpole during a pledge to investigate
back on the soil
bone alchemizes a lighter skeleton for better travel
weight, a myth we tell the kids to give them nightmares
earth, a place we vacation
the ground, a distant cousin we only speak to in the fall,
branches budding from our shoulder blades
feather stems stitched together with love notes
bird chests burgeon so we don't choke on the way up
talons creep out of the places we used to surrender with
we look more monster now than ever before
but weren't we always
at least now we can reap the benefits
instead of meeting the reaper,
arms arch with new purpose
hands up, how we prepare for departure
bullets fade to sparklers
looks like the cop is throwing
us a going away party
fist-fight escalated to a festival

farewell to being foreign

feathers falling all over

an oil spill of cloud dust and flight

soak these new appendages color of new heights

arch upward the way our hands used to

when there was no such thing as escaping

before our bodies gave birth to new appetites

we never look back

this time we know exactly where we come from

know exactly why we left

we're free

no asterisk

nothing up there will ask us why we came

in fact has been waiting for us to leave this place

an *I told you so* exhales from a comet on our way out

we take everything with us

leaving the nothing this world is worth in exchange

future is the only thing we haven't decided yet,

yet, we've decided to go exactly there,

no tomorrow is not promised

but know tomorrow anyone who

wants to take it from us

will have to catch us first

we're going face forward into the unknown

some place

any place

but here.

A NEW PLANET

i've left Earth in search of a new God.
i do not trust the God you have given us.
DANEZ SMITH

And on the first day . . .
Heaven and Earth took off their headphones,
asked where all the rhythm went
heard an escaped black hole strolling the solar system past curfew
blasting Public Enemy, breaking the sound barrier
both plains rotated and caught the universe in orbit
a panther zodiac symbol struck a supernova over the head
with a broken record player
used the needle to shoot up
the sky-
light bled all over the milky way
imagine there was *another* big bang
well this sound was his older brother
they share the same parents
but grew up in different atmospheres

And on the second day . . .
the ground of this new land formed a layer of hydrogen
transformed helium into a livable breath
the people here had fly kicks from jump
rope chains swimming in gold

to keep them down to New Earth
every step a tiny explosion of color
stride a harmony of chain reactions
feet tuned to float before walking
and no, this time,
that is not a metaphor for death,
euphemism for phantom-like feelings
here we float, literally
fully embodied

And on the third day . . .
there was darkness.
period.
and it lived as long as it wanted to
and all the skin it inhabited by it was blessed by the sun
and this new sun promised to never burn it
but even still, on this new globe
being burned, or having a dark (anything) was a compliment
and all the shadow children looked at each other on the playground
and saw god staring back at them
and after recess they returned to a dim classroom
where the teacher, darker than them,
taught them how their skin was a symphony
taught them how self love was the only song they'd need to pass life's
    exam

And on the fourth day . . .
Black God invited her friends over to talk shit about the Old Earth.

And on the fifth day . . .
Old Earth calls someone
to go regulate what sounds like
a party without a curfew
a life missing its roof
a tinted human with the top down
authorities walk the air for days
slip back to gravity empty-handed
say they found nothing or,
there was so much black up there
we couldn't decide whether to kill or take from it

And on the sixth day . . .
Death arrives on this new world with a fruit basket
begs we let bygones be bygones
"a job is just a job," he says
Mike's suicide note caught between his teeth
my grandfather's blood sugar wrapped around his pinky
cloak dripping wet with hashtags
carrying Tracy's cry for help in his eyes,
we take his throat as recompense on sight
without a word or a warning
pass the void from one hand to the next
a response to those who've had the words
snatched right out of their brain midsentence
and their thoughts spread out on the corners of that old earth
we return Death's bones to his parents a whisper
show them the stillness this boy

has forced on our lives
they take him, without question
as if they've learned to expect this expiration

And on the seventh day . . .
that song our parents used to put on
when it was time to clean the house
bellows to every crevice of this place
on the Sabbath we dawn hardwood floors
we remember how joy and Pine-Sol
have a way of lingering in your clothes
hours after you've cleaned the smile off your face
my grandma and your grandma are the fire
we sit around to hear stories from
someone calls us human from afar
we remember a time this word fit
when we subscribed to limits
when we was pretending to be 2 sizes less than
when we was punished for expansion
we cry so hard we leave the stars soaked
collect enough shine from the runoff
to light the whole planet for months
Black God joins us for brunch
it is fresh
we cheer
chalices raised high enough for the sun to sip
love so long our hearts picket for lunch breaks

break nothing that wasn't supposed to
or didn't sign up to shatter before hand
we all write left-handed
this is the only strange thing we see about each other.

BLACK HOUSE

REPRESENTATION FOR
FUTURE REFERENCE

The gate, pending election results, put in her two weeks notice in November
January came around and wasn't nothing keeping us out
instead of a fence, another boundary issued a different name
we adorn the ways we've come to love each other on the outside
barbed wire is laced between every oil painting we've ever owned
all the clowns playing saxophones got the band back together
moved the crew to 1600 Pennsylvania Ave.
feels like home, like we belong there
the front door is now a single entrance guarded by one large man
he is everyone's cousin
holding two sidekicks
all wearing sun glasses
checking ids, but for passage
will accept recitation of
lift every voice and sing
in full without pausing,
or mumbling,
or leaning on your auntie's voice
ladies are always free
inauguration is a block party
doesn't really matter who the president is
or whose name is on the lease

because if the cops come knocking
we will have already moved the party halfway around the world
food prepared by the holiest of hands
happiness home-cooked and heavy
hymns bumping bass so disruptive
a stick of dynamite files a noise complaint
front lawn strewn with ice tea cans and Skittles
looks like a tribute of some kind
except Trayvon is here too
rode in the backseat behind Mike
Rekia picked them up after Sandra decided to walk
they're not late because there was no start time
Aiyana laughs and a bouquet sprouts on her tongue
Aura picks the smallest flower
plants a whole garden in her own throat
on their way past a graveyard
none of them blink, or hold their breath,
don't even know what a graveyard looks like
because on this day we have never died
or had to witness our own closing scene
or had to play the villain after the victim
today we take the fight to the hand that deprives us
instead of pounding the pavement
we bust down the country's door
in place of a seat at the table
we demolish the whole house
distribute the scraps as party favors
grow a neighborhood with no white

anywhere near the things with roots
we know this is only temporary though
night is peeking through the hole in the ozone
sees us having a good ol' time
waiting to have its way with us
the blackest thing we can do is to beat the sun home
tomorrow will return us to dusk, anyway
just before the light issues its last call
we gather for a family photo
so our children will picture themselves here, too
someone slides in the group-chat
they don't know it, but we're doing the same thing again, tomorrow
the house really *is* a home
Luther signed it over to all of us in his will

SAFE MUSIC

IN DEFENSE OF MARVIN GAYE
AND CHUCK BERRY

Some say we got the game on lock
others say the game got a lock on us
got us thinkin' singin' the right key
turn these chains to an accessory
only problem is
you sing a song enough
a remix is bound to happen
careful who you rap around
some snakes steal scales for a living
collect enough samples to feed a pit
careful where you sing,
which direction you spray your voice
some sinks drain pipes for a killing
reinforce these notes in cement
access to the vault restricted
three different sets of melanin detectors
white person enters the black section in a music store
our ancestors follow them around with loaded guns
"steal a note if you want to"
gun cocks
"it'll be the last letter that leaves your body"
let a sound levitate from brown skin

assign it an automatic password
black card necessary for purchase
photo id input to stream our sounds
so what if the genre don't get a shot at awards
only crossover we worry about is the basketball court
where these instrumentals go platinum
dangle from the hoop to make the shots sound better
where the rap battles in the corner
use as much shooting as the athletes
trash talk fills a garbage can no one ever sees get emptied
but knows it'll be hungry again next weekend
no flash photography, we record all our own media
own the rights to the writing and the lighting
what we spend time on is ours, and no one else's.

REINSTATE MY

GRANDMOTHER'S TONGUE

We don't want no more sections in your book
return to us the pages
you ripped from our vertebrae
because of you,
I travel two generations back
only made it around the corner
knocking at my great grandmothers mind
tip of my tongue carrying a basket full of questions like
rumor has it clouds are just fog without a last name,
 Is that why we smoke so much?
Are we looking for a bloodline in the exhaust?
If we inhale hard enough will we spit out an ancestry?
What language did YOUR grandmother speak?
Would you know it if you heard her voice today?
Where's the home for us to go back to?
How do we get there faster?
Is black a nickname for nothing?
suddenly she remembers everything
my mother's first word
the first name we sang post-shackles
the first psalm we walked into an industry
the steps to dances we used to get arrested for
all the answers tsunami her mouth

her voice a waterfall with an attitude

my notebook, now an abyss

her memory a well that never runs out of breath

The cure for chest cavities is a sweet heart

Love heals all the spaces people chew in us

I sit across the table content

listening,

to every word,

pen practicing double dutch

jumping in between lines

We've always had our backs against the ropes,

we whip ass though

even when the ropes was against our backs

her grin is a butterfly in this fleeting moment

my hand flapping in the wind furiously

trying to keep up stream,

swimming one sentence at a time

writing,

so I will have answers to pour into my own family one day.

HANDWRITTEN APOLOGY

FROM THE GOVERNMENT

~~To whom it may concern~~

~~Hello All,~~

Dear Black People,

~~We fucked up.~~

We are still fucking up.

Enclosed you will find a blank check.

This doesn't makeup for ~~what those people did~~

what we are still doing.

We had no idea ~~you would still care~~ you would survive this long.

We hope you will use the money to ~~leave and never return~~ buy

back your freedom.

Pay all you like, truth is we ~~don't have it~~ never had it.

Spend the money ~~wisely~~ however you see fit.

G.O.J.F.

Get

Outta

Jail

Free

No government should have a monopoly on labor.

No game piece should spend life in a box for cutting corners.

No difference in a board game and board room.

Same lives getting played with by people trading properties.

FORECAST FOR FOOD DESERTS

Imagine a cold day
where the wind keeps its offspring from playing outside
sitting around the fire
weatherman takes the day off
all the bad things stay home from school
call into work sick
arc occupied for 24 hours
newscaster reports
change in climate shows that a storm of golden, cream-filled cakes
is going to strike all the shady parts of the U.S. today
Twinkie wrappers start to sprinkle the hood
diabetes files for unemployment
understands the only way this will work is if he doesn't
first pastry splatters on the west side of Akron
next shower appears in Detroit
then Jackson
then Oakland
then Atlanta
then Cleveland
then New Orleans
then Baltimore
and so on
and so on this day
we eat
until full,
and empty is a relationship

we can't remember why we

ever got attached to

we eat

one bite for every day we've had to choose this meal in place of

parents

we eat

swallow knowing there is plenty more where this came from

holding back nothing because our siblings got their fill first

we eat

eyes flutter a gleam that would make a firefly blush

we eat

because biting is now the most violent thing we know how to do

we eat

and don't think about the water we waded

or the nooses we drowned in

or the desks we disappeared behind to put food on the table

we eat

one pillow-filled taste after another

we aren't counting portions

no one is timing the feast

and in this moment,

nothing else matters,

no underlying racial tension

between the color of the cakes

and the cream inside

or how all good things are painted white

right now,

we are *just* eating junk food.

TREES WITHOUT BRANCHES

buildings without erasers
pencils without escape plans
ink that doesn't stain
but never leaves
wood without wrinkles
ceilings without stretch marks
castles without corrosion
kings without corners
intersections without accidents
blueprints that don't fold for a price
dreams without floor plans
the freedom to fall
and never taste smashing
fear without guns
anger without triggers
two birds without stones
black folks without targets
bullets without preferences
or premeditated destinations
or a taste for charcoal
diamonds without blood
lower-cases without capitalism
a lived life without a hyphen
a breath without abbreviation
space to live, fully articulated, without choking.

P I

Three Points
one for
freedom to travel
two for the centuries floating in purgatory
adjust the score whichever way the decimal migrates
or the wind blows
or the cotton crumbles
or the knot slips
or the open-ended question regurgitates
throw-up the wrong continent and yesterday
might snatch your customs out of thin air
might pull your heritage out the front seat of the car
drag your history onto a freeway and let the sparks fly
might call it a holiday
"where you from?"
"what plantation you rep?"
spit up the wrong set
baby you wont make it to the crib
make a mess at the protest
watch them kidnap you out ya high chair
dangle a rope around ya neck that's not a bib
who raised you?
don't you know that tantrum is a lethal offense
too much noise get you in time-out
or took out the game permanently

put in a penalty box for defending people
born in the same color jersey as you
"other" a square most roots can't live in
let alone see a check from it
how the political correct an outsider
corner them into a label
no need to id the body
when the body was stripped of its identity while living,
just an "other"
we teach our toddlers to avoid the same patterns
that got our neighbors took out the sequence
our existence an irrational number
how we never see an end coming
but know it exists,
somewhere to the alt-right of control,
down the dark alley of some calculating menace
around a brick corner page in a gentrified notebook
in the back pocket of a political prison,
waiting,
to have our numbers crunched,
pattern, how we learn survival
so, perhaps something that doesn't
repeat is not that the best option
how else will we predict being sliced
and avoid serving life in the pan.

AN ENDING THAT MAKES SENSE

(DRY SNITCHING ON MAURICE)

When I was 13 me and my best friend tried to steal a broomstick
that didn't belong to us from someone else's lair
a witch teleported to her porch across the street,
cursed our cauldron skin,
banished us back to the black neighborhood we withdrew from,
the spell kicked in immediately,
I only lived two blocks away at the time
but the effects were so powerful
I retreated to the next village over because it felt like I belonged there,
because I believed when she told me to go back where I came from,
we learn to escape at an early age
generations of dissipation passed down
from our fathers and the trees that raised them
my uncle once laughed so hard a bullet carried him out in a casket
his dad was so good at dissolving some say he never existed,
my aunt know invisibility too
taught my cousin how to see right through me,
now,
if we could get our hands on the *good* stuff
we lack the ability to shapeshift, become anew in an instant
the illusion that transforms mass shooters into misunderstood gamers
you know the way a headline performs metamorphosis
remodel a lifeless skeleton into a hulk-like demon

how our spirit go from homeless to haunting in the blink of a body cam
how we get murdered then subpoenaed to show in court for our own
    defense
how the most credible witness is also the one who can no longer speak
we want the potion that controls prison proportions
we demand the cloak that allows us safe passage
home after red and blue lights flash
that old enchantment the
constitution cast blew right past us
so we need them ingredients
we'll spice up the recipe
bring the right seasonings
make a curse of our own,
pin safety to our bones
a juxtaposition to the original jinx
where we be the exception
never have to be *twice as* NOTHING
cuz our singular does the trick
—poof—
Barbara gets her house back
—poof—
a dragon exhales and burns the head off of all the confederate statues
—poof—
anybody who reaches for a gun turns into glitter
—poof—
in a rare turn of events,
black boy dies,
we all mourn the loss.

the end.

—poof—

black bear is returned her cub

folded neatly on the front porch

not a crease out of place

all the black boys

march the neighborhood half-mast

not a single file out of order

—poof—

at a moment's notice, we are gone

whole heartbeats in tact

just making music somewhere

the credits roll exactly when they're supposed to.

REINVENTION OF THE WHEEL

PROTEST AS AN ACCEPTED FORM
OF COMMUNITY SERVICE

A round is no more another shape
than a body is able to defend
its name after having its pulse removed
I bring my "ACAB" sign to my probation officer
as proof I've spent my mandatory hours correctly
she adds another charge to my court fees
I protest the payment and lose more freedom
a leash is no less restraining
simply because it stretches
only makes it so we forget
for a moment, until yanked by the collar bone
I am asked to perform for a room
full of faces that line pockets
the same year I am threatened
with suspension for using my voice
a rebellion is no more a riot
than a nickname can recall birth
than two parents can refute DNA
resistance is an imperfect science
made to disrupt gestation periods
throw a rock in a washer machine
worst case the cycle starts over

best case an entirely new
machine is built to replace it
if not for how we take off work
put on hard hats to deconstruct
demolish pinnacles protected by pigs
demand trash be removed from patrols
involuntarily direct action to injustice
a man loses his eye to a wooden bullet
receives a citation instead of worker's comp.
we volunteer martyrs put on our
clothes same as anyone else with a soul
one strapless boot after the other
one left wing at a time
fly in circles, sure
how else would we make a tornado
or produce enough wind
to blow this unstable structure down.

AFFORDABLE SKIN CARE

Black don't crack cuz the whip did
former engineers mastered track marks
then crack sold faster than whips did
coke ain't hit the hood til they whipped it
rocks rolled onto the streets encrypted
dressed as another ailment
we called them junkies
instead of test subjects
unknown villains instead of unknowing volunteers
pipes burst
addiction spilled onto every floor of the house
broken glass and shattered families
boys finding pieces of their fathers splayed all over cracks in the sidewalk
moisturize these memories a smooth sentiment
acknowledge the ash,
or white powder gathered in an area of dry skin
so deprived of its needs
it starts attacking itself for more attention
in the most severe cases
the ash has to be surgically removed from the body,
addiction becomes a part of you in that way
a problem shows up so often you know what to reach for
this white substance
the body now believes it can't live without

"apply as needed,"
eventually application
is necessary to leave the house
or to leave the bed of cinder
where a hospital once was.

PLOT TWISTS

SUMMARY

A horror movie where the black person not only lives,
but is the monster,
gets to come back for all the sequels
plays himself in the TV adaptation of the thriller
if you think about it,
beast was always the safest role
only character guaranteed to appear in every version
even when the actor moves on, or is too old for a remake
the killer remains
evil, yes
but alive nonetheless
chased down,
hunted with pitch forks
might die for things he didn't do
same as real life
but in this scenario,
there's always a sequel

SCENE

a commercial for bleach
airs during the super bowl
there is no racial undertone in sight

not even with a microscope

not even a fine-tooth anchorman

can comb a controversy

SCENE

hooded figure walks down suburban boulevard

pockets for hands

gloom where a face would be

legs a whole mess of suspicious

business casual couple collapses out of bar

fumbling 2-body mass everywhere

next destination a blur,

sloppily they stumble in the direction of the hoodie

they notice the color of his consequence

Channel 7 told them what a color that bold

does to people on nights like this

out in the open

still they were desperate for a way out

there!

between the cacophony of cars zooming past

another footpath just like this one, minus the fear

a safe escape from this unidentified figure

before they can make a move, though

the street crosses them

opening in the road hiccups their feet into a pond of prejudice

they emerge as one thing

one display of bias

one barely moving organism
the hooded figure
who now fears for *his* life
sidesteps this pile of filth in his way.

SCENE

dark alley (v.s.) white ally
alley walks into a store the ally owns
alley has no idea what to buy
just knows how much space he has inside
ally does not see the alley enter the store
instead of a shadow the ally chooses to see no one
nothing happens
a silhouette with a badge finds his way inside
has already decided who his weapon would shed light in
knows exactly which surface is getting drawn on
reaches for lighting utensil
before the shimmering starts
alley looks the ally dead in the pocket
a safety pin catches the eye
thank god!
safety pin leaps from the clothing of the ally
christened in white tears
dawning an "all lives" cape
as he flies into action
gun glistens right past the safety pin
light ruptures the alley without flinching

drenches the whole store in dark spots

the safety pin,

ashamed,

flustered,

flush with frustration,

falls aimlessly to the floor

the ally looks up from the register

just in time to see a dead thing,

sheds a tear for the safety pin,

realizes she actually didn't lose anything,

prepares the store for the next customer

SCENE

before professional athletes stream onto court

the flag stands before the mic preparing to pledge allegiance to the
  people

stares into a sea of unimpressed herds

a "bout time!" slings from the throat of a sheep in the front row

a single blood-colored bead forms around the stars' neck

the stripes tremble, legs weak from all the marching

catch a side-eye from a team of retired picket signs

a note tries to creep from the flag's lips,

before its mouth can muster the strength

the flag falls under pressure

cannot sing

or salute

kneeling is the best that the flag can do,

the people, and the cottonmouth workers they came to see

all kneel in solidarity

slave owner presses the PA button

but the mic takes the words right out of his mouth

buries them in a pile of dirty towels by the locker room

in an interview following the game

the mic remarked,

there was nothing left to say,

the action spoke louder than words.

WAVES

WATERPROOF DURAGS AND HEADWRAPS

We square up with a tragedy

shadow box an eclipse

live so many storms

disaster is natural

how we speak to relatives in different borders

last time we crossed an ocean we lost some molecules

we realized this liquid be the only thing indestructible

live in cycles instead of dying

and we've been liquid for longer than we knew

we fill space, no stranger to withholding outpouring into the concrete

you ever try to swallow a river out of spite?

swell up your chest to challenge a tidal wave?

we choose this form of fierce

become that which drowned Katrina

how justified would we be to hurricane a whole land mass

to reduce this hemisphere to a shoreline

are we not within our rights to start again?

consider every piece of dehydrated land a gift

a show of self-discipline

be thankful, revere in this mercy

how in this new body of water

we simply take solace in being left at bay

instead of suffocating this rock whole

breathing is no longer an inside joke

we splash laughter on for stale humor

existing no more a second-hand language

a trade we learn if we pay attention to how our elders

trickled so long without evaporating completely

now we drip

cascade

without borders

or any hard thing, stopping our flow

absorbed into every living aspect,

they, would literally have to end the world to get rid of us.

NO MORE LISTS

& no more counting

& no more numbered days

& no more protest

& no more mourning

& no more sons falling before their time

& no more stars casting shadows

& no more reason to get nervous at a traffic stop

& no more traffic stop

& no more cliff hangers

& no more stories left unwritten

& no more ghost writers

& no more pigeon-holing futures

& no more skin-affiliated forms of success

& no more would-have

& another thing

& another thing after that

& however many more things we decide we deserve

& tongue that gets tired of introductions in past tense

& past tense that refuses to show up to dinner unannounced

& families who don't know any ghosts on a first name basis

& first names that never go out of style

& never find hashtags fashionable

& fashion that don't get you dead

& eyes without weapons

& looks that can't kill

& no more poems about black death

RESOLUTION

A LEGALLY BINDING AGREEMENT

Whereas finders have been keepers, even if what they found was not
  lost
Whereas whatever left the loser's weeping swept across a continent
Whereas broom swept until only a pile of dust remained
Whereas an old world was force-fed a new name
Whereas whoever didn't like the taste was alleviated of their voice
Whereas resistance to the new flavor became a diagnosed illness
Whereas genocide cured all symptoms,
The same way acid washes clean,
Whereas the first natural disaster was erasure
Whereas the rubber was so good at its job
you could hardly tell there was anything on the paper
except for white to begin with
Whereas the paper started to believe its own lie
Whereas the paper's children inherited all its folds
POINT OF INFORMATION: the only difference between a fold and a
  wrinkle is how hard it is to forget
Whereas a country's economy evolved faster than a conscience
Whereas the chains weren't so much destroyed as they were
  softened into new ways of holding
POINT OF INFORMATION: nicknaming a weapon doesn't change
  what it was made to do
  a.) gifting "property" your last name doesn't change what you
    made them do

RESOLVED: those who shall not be named because the name has been
      printed on all the towers,
lose all rights to the aforementioned names and towers
RESOLVED: "they" shall hence forth be referred to as no one,
as in, no one came and stole a country,
now no one cares,
no one is trying to figure out where all the color went,
after no one admits the white out was intentional
no one takes responsibility for their actions,
no one is willing to give back what was taken
so we who shall not be mentioned in history books,
take it all, back.

REVOLUTION

A MAGICALLY BINDING AGREEMENT

Bullet leaves barrel
in search of flesh
prefers a human
finds brown skin
close enough
crab with no shell
hoodie made of quicksand
bushel of burrowing waiting to happen
a weed with a pulse and no roots
growing somewhere
it doesn't belong
in a greenhouse,
instead of a burial plot
bullet bolts to make lightning
of the bones
just before contact, the body
develops an automatic allergy
sneezes instantly then
depletes into dandelions
seeds fly in all directions
stem spine so elastic
how it bends for survival
reflex

the same plant

sprouts a new address

sends the soul across town

bullet, confused and dismayed,

returns to the front door of the gun

stomach empty

metal hungry and unfulfilled

intestines a puzzle

amazed of its vacancy

no black anywhere near its tongue

and no one dies

and no one died

and no *one* color

is the source

of all the funerals anymore

or hogging the afterlife

and no one minds the pollen, everywhere

OUTRO (A BETTER DJ)

If there is any salvation
let it be at a basement party in Ypsilanti
103 degrees inside on a Thursday night in Autumn
trees dressed to impress
lingerie made of leaves
one hard shake away from naked
red & orange tap-dancing the grass
knowing this chill is the last song
before the season changes playlists
somewhere in the Midwest
after the last class of the week
we flood into the streets
flow for the apartments with the least space
but the most attractive sermon tonight
we arrive in our weekend's best
miles from the sea nowhere near a church
walls witnessing a Jericho of jubilation
penance paid for entry,
unless you know the pastor personally
unless the deacon could sneak you in through the back
while happy birthday hymnal is humming from the kitchen
best not be late,
lest you miss communion
ceremony of collecting bread to pay for libations
miracle how the host turns paper into wine,

rolls verses into smoke

lighter flicks

a freestyle spreads like wildfire

DJ taking no request for the pulpit

knows to tailor his message based on how we worship

stuffed together perspiring all our sins

lines blur between whose moist is whose

doing things we will deny once the lights come up

but let this darkness last a lifetime

even if we never find the words

may our bodies forever know the lyrics and move accordingly

on the Southside of some abandoned track

in the backyard of an overused ad-lib

time stops moving long enough for us to collide a chorus

through clasped hands we pray to the aux cord

that the next choir the speakers play be a blessing

blessed be the organs we play roulette with

the pipes the alcohol accompanies most

holy be the dance floor that protect us from the warzone

praise the beats that machine gun our self conscience

we know of trap music,

the way a fish knows worms ain't got no business underwater

but somehow still falls for the hook every time

here packed in this living room like sardines

capture our flailing

neck deep in an ocean of our own sweat

shore enough to drown before the tide comes

sand enough to rebuild everything we lose in the swag surfin' leave the shells in a rap song

save the slugs and preserve this habitat

listen close enough you can hear pain drying

we've accepted the tables won't turn

so leave us the turntables

let us scratch and mix our criminal records

if we have to die,

let it be at 3 a.m.

after the music stops

after the liquor store closes

after the last rotation finds stillness

and there is no more basement to belong in.

LEGALIZED GATHERING

Imagine no one getting smoked when the cops roll up
ashes don't have to return to ashes
but now vanish into any imaginable object
reincarnate as a paper plane with one passenger
fly until the smog runs out
come back to life in a cypher
spit ball into a cemetery
spin backwards atop a lighter
backflip off a burned thumb
inhale a horizon
reverse tail spin a shotgun
exhale a kaleidoscope
dispense dope diction
dispel rope fiction
hang as long as we want to
choke, cough a lynching
diagnose us diaspora,
homesick, whole as any circle can be.

A HAPPY HOLIDAY

What is the 4th of July to a _____?
Low hanging fruit
from a rotting government branch
selectively feeding citizens
just enough to avoid malnutrition
show me a crop, or an image of a black
public figure with all their edges in place
that didn't catch a bullet to the Adam's apple
gift me a snake without blood on its wrapping
show me an evening that beat the odds
show me a savior the gov't didn't crucify
then tell us it was ok to worship him
after they'd made him holy
punctured every decision he ever made,
what to a fragment, is February
but another reminder of being incomplete
a memorial to the halves we be
a testament to the scatter plot we are
a dishonorable discharge from the past
what is the pledge of allegiance to a wounded knee
but an anthem to scraped skin
sticks and stones broke bones
but words ain't never healed you
but transformed a genocide into a day off,
label us our own nativity scene

a revolutionary religion,

how we die on the cross-walking

enter the sky-boxing

buy front seats to our death on the big screen

resurrect into a burial

3 days after the cop is removed from the public's sanctuary

the priest hasn't spoken on the injustice, yet

congregation stopped lining his pockets,

now the doors of the church are open

except its service is no longer needed,

we believe in ourselves now,

know there is a heaven in our home-cooked meals

know we have been our salvation from the beginning,

how we feed a multitude with no fresh food in 6-mile radius

how we change contaminated water into a myriad of boxed
lunches

how we pedal hope, and repeat the cycle,

how we grow

against the grain

and still take time off

to celebrate.

VOICE IN THE AUCTION

When our blood stains your uniform
They will paint you a war hero
That's where America got its colors from
Red, on Whites, in Blue

Poor portrayals patrol a block into a museum
statues posted on every corner
curator pushing canvas for the low
pounds of white for next to nothing
nothing lives where buildings used to
empty space is buying up all the property
artists have lost everything
was better off when the world saw no beauty in their abstract
when you could call a spade and spade
no one was a re-nigger
fiends fold into caricatures
animated approximations of who they once were
addiction is somehow a metaphor
the rich bury into artistic expression
handguns outnumber fathers 9 to 1
if we could sell a fragmented building back for a profit
take a picture of our own poverty
and convince the public it was distant
we'd make a killing
into a concept,

because this type of problem is always better in another country

somewhere intangible

we remain untouched anyway,

let us convince you the jungle is not concrete

that the beasts here came from another habitat, too

proof pigs have no respect for someone else's farm

graffiti was born that way

won't have to pretend the artist is dead

because he probably is

spiking the value of this masterpiece

but ain't that why they buy up these places anyway

mistake the blood stains for a symbol

see artists "misusing" their talents

criminalize the creation

collect the places we grew up in

forget to catalogue the living rooms

the simple lives the apartment complex displaces

pour destitution into the edge of a busted pallet,

purchase this imagery

pay the price in full

enough to reinvent black wall street

patent preservation

picture a bombing in reverse

aggressively rebuilding what you did not destroy

post this depiction in a haunted house

so the ghosts can feel more at home.

PROPERTY

FOR JOSH WILLIAMS

Ain't Black lives just property
ain't we born with blank price tags on our skin
ain't officers really just customers who mean to take half off
don't the cashier court system forget
to charge the killer on his way out the store
but charge the item for spilling blood on the cop's clothing
ain't we all just property anyway?
when we *was* possession,
didn't they at least make "people" pay a fine for killing us
said there was damage done to their goods,
ain't life a shelf we aren't supposed to be on
ain't we all just property anyway?
don't they change our label for their benefit,
white man sees no black, no boy
sees hulk-like demon in Ferguson
sends it back to hell before the demon can say hello,
the lifeless body cooks in the sun for hours,
white man receives no jail time,
in response, black boy burns building
black boy sentenced to 8 years in prison,
when police bullets burn through black skin,
then black skin burns building,

ain't the building the victim,

won't these broken windows get a better

public defender than a broken black boy?

System says,

building benefit us more, building make us money

black people been broke

U.S. breaking the ain't no different

we subtractin' a deficit killing them ain't no difference

ain't math universal

ain't what happens to one side

supposed to happen to the other?

Ain't the pledge of allegiance an unbalanced equation

ain't justice an addition for sum?

Ain't we all incomplete numbers

don't black boys resemble decimals

is that why they keep rounding them up

ain't they quick to call the protest a riot

to mourn the property,

won't call it murder though,

hold funerals for spray painted sidewalks

quicker than they hold cops accountable

don't we get tickets for stopping traffic

ain't we sent to jail for disruptions

don't they call it littering when we leave our signs in the street

but they left Mike there for 4½ hours

some say he's still laying there

don't they clean animals off the highway quicker than that?

ain't we breathin' enough to at least be animal

but ain't it safer for us to just be a thing?
when a building falls and breaks the sidewalk
no part of the building gets arrested
won't we stop going to jail for
defacing property if we just become it?

40 ACRES AND A MULE

Right outside the courtroom
a crying mother holds a remnant of her son
so close the tears never actually leave her face
faces the fact her child will now know this captivity, too
same as the tears
outside of his own body
no idea where to go next
no way to go back where he came from
salty and evaporating quickly
the lake on this mother's face
sows a seed in her palms
which she returns to the land
plans to grow a whole field of her suns
in a green glass house with a roof
made of something else
maybe plastic
so they can shape whatever's ahead of them
maybe no house at all and no address
maybe this time no one will come looking for them
but what if they never grow, or worse
what if they grow so good another farmer notices
maybe planting is the worst thing to do
wasn't harvest what took her son in the first place
some gun on a dim-lit road
looking to end its own famine

saw the boy as a way out
made a snack of his insides
ricocheted between bones,
and licked the body clean
left no trace of the mayhem
back on the farm, all that's left is this mother
pulling along this weight,
of knowing whatever she grows
may end up feeding the same animals
that starved her womb into a drought.

NEWTON'S THIRD LAW PASSED

Rules: We get two black people
for every one white person not indicted.
Or every bad thing that happens
to a black person, happens opposite, twice.
Or black privilege is a real thing now.

Cop that "wasn't *trained* properly" stops a black body dead in its
tracks.
  Two black bodies grow where the blood falls.
My aunt loses her house in a fire.
  *My father gets his father back and peach cobbler rains from the
  heavens.*
Black girl "doesn't fit" criteria for a job.
  *Floats out of interview owning the company and Barack gets
  another term in office.*
You give one of us life in prison.
  *We give Malcolm his life back and his former widow shoots the faces
  off of Mt. Rushmore.*
White person publishes a book on reverse racism.
  *Racism actually reverses and Chance the Rapper rewrites the
  constitution.*
Rent money plays hide and seek with my cousin's pockets.
  *Fred Hampton spends the night at a friend's house on the night in
  question raises his own sun and solar power never goes out of style.*

Pot curses the kettle's black.

> *Kettle boils the pot's tongue into a soup then feeds the whole*
> *neighborhood and Kool Aid releases packets with the perfect amount*
> *of sugar included.*

I am followed around for suspicion of shopping.

> *Assata gets a teaching position with tenure and a license to live hangs*
> *on the wall in her office.*

For every wrongdoing

> *there is an equally opposite reaction.*

TYPE OF QUIET YOU CAN

RAISE A FAMILY ON

Next to fingers
jack-hammering on a keyboard
a ball of fur sleeps his life away
every breath enters and exits the fuzz
the silence is enough to hang a grudge with
fingers stop tapping
unfasten prints from the casket carrying words to screen
to stare at this living
this dog, sleeping
animal by all means
open to attack from all angles
somehow choosing obliviousness
the fingers
really the skin attached to them,
envy what it must feel like
to be safe enough to sleep in open spaces
without fear someone will see you
and take your weight,
a pound of your bark
or what your skin's sound might do to property value
or how the color of your branches
falling all over town
might scare the visitors away

might mistake you garbage and
leave you a pile of dried choices in another's yard
until a helping hand
rakes you into a black bag
here, on this floor that is surely someone else's
the fur has all its needs met
we want, whatever that is
the frivolous flight
fierce fading of feeling a fight
aggressive need, for stillness
call it a nap if you must
a moment so quiet
we can afford, finally
to be unconscious.

A CHANCE AT REDEMPTION

Come now and repent
lay your (not so) great granddaddy's sins at our feet
you own his land
now own his iniquity
confess your guilt by association
leave out one ill
and be written from existence
we hold the pen and the power to retell
pray we don't run out of ink & thirst your blood for art,
pray our wrath be gone with the wind
build a monument,
or we will cleanse this world of you,
an arc won't save you
no need to split the water
in search of the ancestors you left afloat
nor sacrifice your seed to satisfy our sweet tooth
if you convince us further of your unworthiness
we will simply snap our fingers
put two cosmos together
and flicker you into dust
forget you ever burned
flame a universe to replace you with ash
phoenix an Armageddon
our anger is no longer a stereotype
we tip-toe away from in public
unleash in small doses
for fear of being capped

all this uproar

now a cause for admiration

marvel at this might

no holding back

doesn't matter what you call us now

your words mean little to us as they ever did

useless as throwing salt at an ocean

everybody wins though,

you wanted us without breath and pulse

good news, we are no longer alive,

but also now cannot die

we know you love to be predator

so pray,

now *to* us, instead of *on* us

get on your knees,

hands raised in surrender

off-beat worship & all

alter your egos

sculpt your mouth in our praises

gather in masses

spread the gospel of your guilt

in equal doses 400 times a day

truth is this wrath may never end

least not in your life span

be patient though, these things take time

we have centuries to make up for

if you're lucky

one day, our will

will be done.

CHEAP CAPES OR THE MONEY

TO SAVE OURSELVES (S.O.S.)

A hero looks out over a city he couldn't save,

a gutless Gotham stares at itself in a cracked window,

the ashes of a tragic love story are spray-painted on the backhand

    of the tallest building,

it wears a clock to cover up the scars,

its friends call it a watch tower to keep

the neighbors from asking questions,

a cremation was recycled into an exposition,

the whole block avoids eye contact with the erosion,

pretends the abuse was art,

paints the house's protruding stomach as intentional,

crops a food desert into a necessary image of the struggle,

suddenly we believe there's color in dying,

how death is short-lived,

but still eventful enough to be illustrated,

art and atrocity wear then same tongues in conversation

color-code-switching camera men came

to catalogue the corrosion

made an exhibit of the endangered species

now they need somewhere to display the dead

I mean hang the photos

suddenly studios erect in places the city swore could grow nothing,

abandoned buildings are failing organs in the body of a dying city, dying buildings are abandoned organs failing the city's body,

doctor changes his name to landlord,

landlord does not operate,

only diagnoses,

either way refuses to treat the patient,

also refuses ownership of what decay is sure to follow,

quietly the life expires into vacancy,

the coroner narrows the cause of death to health insurance, or rent,

or greed so infectious the parasite risked its own life for a better feast,

neighboring structures soon suffer the same fate,

their deaths are much less painful,

boulders are born from buildings

gravel/gargoyles gawking/goblins groveling

rubble and lava where the streets used to meet for lunch

seconds before the last igneous spec

is burned from his dormancy

the hero rises from the rocks

where the corner store used to stand

drives a knife through a stack of eviction notices

an almost hollow city builds a case against the vacuums

families settle out of court for malpractice,

use the money to hire doctors that look like them

who have an investment in making sure the property does not die

treatment starts,

after only a few weeks of self-love

all the cells of the old sickness, let's call them "white blood",

are nowhere to be found

vacate every construction site in the immediate area

the whole internal structure is rewired

in preparation for the unveiling

a whole new skeleton was built

but it looks like nothing changed

because this time, it didn't

the black neighborhood was remodeled with all its black in tact

the shadows stayed attached to the buildings

they grew up in

outsiders wanted to build a neighborhood that was

to die for.

but this one

and its dying

is just fine

without them.

none of the dark parts of the city

were harmed in the making of this metropolis

PARENTAL RIGHTS TO

OUR OWN LANGUAGE

White person says nigga
& this is no different from how the sword was forged
except the face exclaims the sharp edges don't cut anymore
ain't that a privilege in itself
to know exactly where you come from
then choose to pretend amnesia
to perform forgetting,
feign not knowing
as if your family hadn't used
that weapon to separate
slice/solicit shame/silence/shackle/sham superiority
the word feels right at home
as it should
this mouth be the first house it knew,
still,
allow us to redecorate.
instructions to the artist:
make a fist,
call it a paintbrush,
your arm, a tool for expression
this jaw a can of paint
a jar of "just kidding"
cover the walls red

flood the ceiling in this wet

furnish the curtains a new tongue

the word will not recognize this

former place of residence

a mangled shell is no place for an adjective

let it wander the streets

until hunger consumes it

or an empty so strong

the word itself desires being eaten

leads the sword to those he once sought to destroy

chew the two syllables unrecognizable

spit them back transformed a place holder

rearrange its purpose in life

the sword is now just words

no one will question how we adopt this child

raise him to do new things

vaccinate our young in this expression

be damned if someone outside our family

claims ownership of him now

the word is ours

we have the proper documents,

and matching bite marks to prove it.

A SERIES OF SHORT STORIES

ABOUT WHITE PEOPLE

NON-FICTION

For the sake of not generalizing an entire race,
playing the role of all white people will be "white person"

white teacher(person) mispronounces a black name
three of five days of the week,
consoles the student by assuring them
that ⅗ is better than nothing

white person touches black hair for the 13th time this week
and an ancestor steps up out her grave looking for revenge
14th time ancestor brings her family with her to the fight
white person touches black hair for the 15th time and pulls
back an amendment, unable to comprehend another's freedom
white person reaches again
this time the hair forms into a rebellion
and takes the hand prisoner,
startled at the sheer animosity of the curls
the uncivilized behavior of the kinks
 white person nicknames the hair savage,

white person conquers an island and calls it a vacation
white person steals your phone and then helps you look for it

white person steals your home
then tells you its cold outside

white person walks into bar-
and no one sticks around
for the punchline cuz drunk white people aren't funny,

white person puts on a uniform,
forgets to remove his white sheet,
burns a cross down into a handgun
then patrols the streets doing the Lord's work
white person is a ghost,
looking to escort very specific
colors of people to the afterlife
white supremacy loves company
long as the company knows its place
in the backyard, and chained
where no one can hear the company demand
equal treatment, or a seat at the dinner table

white person never murders people of color
can't kill what you don't consider alive to begin with
white person never thug, never riot, only troubled
white person in trouble is simply a person
without their needs met, white person always need
always hungry, always opening neighbor's fridge without permission
always jaw open ready to bite off the most appetizing culture

white person is loud at a protest,
but silent at the dinner table with racist family,
white person hold flag as heritage celebration,
"forgets" the part in history where the flag lost,
"forgets" the flag didn't want to be American in the first place,

white person sneeze or bump you but don't excuse them-self,
white person wish god's blessings on the same bodies they stole
    religion from,
white person force religion on the same land they stole bodies from
white person has fingerprint in all the dirt of this world
with soiled hands
still writes stories
in a way that sounds
like everyone *else*
is in need of cleansing

A CRACKED MIRROR FOR GOOD LUCK

When I look in the mirror I see hope
I see black and boy in the same frame
I see firecracker eyeballs
I see sparklers for fists
might look dangerous
but never hurt no body
I see dormant volcano
they see an eruption
I see a sidewalk
they see a potential Pompeii
I see law abiding citizen
they see a criminal in human skin
I see reaching for license
they see an explosion
they see an aftermath
they see the ghost of a chalk outline
they see a threat where none exists
I see another shadow lost its life today
because they didn't see a pulse behind the melanin
or thought the heartbeat was stolen from a more
deserving skin tone
if I walk a little further
I see a protest
I see a grieving body of people
they see a riot

they see a road block
they see something delaying their way home
we see cop lights, don't know if we'll make it home
I see myself at a traffic stop and sight stops working
I don't see life, I don't see future,
I don't see why I was pulled over
but I feel blood racing, I feel jitters
I feel parts of my anatomy I never knew existed
preparing to pack their bags and leave me in the driver seat
he sees me nervous, thinks my black is hiding something
flashlight searches the car without permission
sight comes back
cars drive past
not sure they see
what's about to happen
I see him reach for a gun
I see a flash
can't tell if it's a gunshot
or another cop pulling up
I don't see a difference
I don't hear a bang
but I smell death's
fingertips reach into
the window next to-
I see my license again
I see myself driving home
this morning I woke up I had to wait hours
before I looked like I thought I did

this morning my face felt like it was trying

on clothes that didn't belong to it

this morning my sight is a filter

this morning what *"they see"* is an adopted son who lives in my eyelids

this morning a stereotype saw me in the mirror

he told me,

we're not leaving the house, until one of us changes

otherwise, neither of us is going to make it back.

CLEAR DANCE FLOOR

FOR BLACK BOYS WHO CAN'T SIT STILL

Dance is the safest way to travel when you're always a target
Rodney King was the first music video
to go viral solely for the beat
music videos are where Black boys perfect dark magic safely
away from the weight of bench pressing stereotypes
we can do with our bodies whatever we want
and it ain't so much a dance
as it is a reclaiming of land
we was told was never ours to begin with
I learned how to moonwalk next to a vacuum
and I still take steps back when life sucks
in 6th grade I learned that my body was a sermon
I learned how to pray with my feet
back when dance was the only religion we had faith in
I was baptized sliding backwards at a talent show
Mom says my life is still headed in the wrong direction
I thought it was fun, didn't know I was preparing for battle
some say the Thriller video zombie
is the last time they saw Michael Jackson
black in public
wouldn't you change your skin
if you found out the world only loved
the dancing zombie video

because the black boy was already dead

because he slid across the screen with his hands up

wasn't that the first time we saw brown skin waste

away to a rhythm, but called it pop music

Trayvon Martin was a remix with no features

George misread the title thought it said *"No Future"*

Mike Brown was an *a cappella* sample of the same song

they snatchin' kings and collecting royalties

I used to believe that I could dodge bullets if I practiced hard enough

before I knew my father could breakdance

I knew the cold silence that accompanied a traffic stop,

the chemical imbalance I felt when hearing sirens

I knew the choreography to keeping my hands visible in case of

    combustion

how the wrong move could lead to me never dancing again

the day a cop told me I didn't belong in a neighborhood I grew legs in

my tongue was a wet fuse

my voice, a pinned grade

my fists were nuclear missiles

his mouth pressing launch codes

my body knew it was supposed to explode

but didn't know why

that night I danced in an evacuated parking lot

for two hours just to avoid detonating

and I think all us Black boys fall into bomb-making this way

as an attempt to diffuse a weapon we inherited

Black boys dance to show that our bloodstream is jet fuel

to prove that our spines be rocket ship

besides, what threat can America make
against a body that has already proven
it will blow up on command
I never asked my dad about this first
time he made his anatomy into a land mine
I just assumed he was triggered
or went through something that
made him replace his joints with fireworks
I figured he knew one day a cop was going to
throw him to the ground
I thought breakdance was his way of
practicing what to do when he got there
the next time you see a Black boy shake so hard
you think his back's broken
consider, that we break our bones
just to prove we are in control of them
don't ask *why you always dancin'?*
ask,
what kind of country, makes it people
feel like they're safest when moving?
We dance cuz bein' Black is stressful
we dance because after a long day
sometimes defying gravity is the only
rebellious thing we have time to do
we dance cuz you can't hit what you can't catch
our dance is alluding to war zone our dance is a form of combat
ever so often, I have flashbacks to the battles
when I get too drunk to remember that I'm not a soldier anymore

or the music is just intoxicating enough for me not to care
in those moments, I remember the living room
I turned into a training camp
make my limbs into a bomb shelter
and let the beat, blow me away.

SUPER HUMAN POWER

Luke Cage is the hero we've been waiting for,
a killer cop's worst nightmare
America's greatest fear
a black body, that cannot be broken,
a midnight marvel man impervious to attack
but we've seen this kind of mutant resistance stamped out before
when the Black Panthers fashioned black power fists into trigger
    fingers
the United States disarmed them
separated the organization at the joint
made sure the skeleton was buried without a headstone
I don't want to be invincible, nor bullet proof
I fear this place would only dedicate its time to
finding new ways of killing me anyway
but since you asked,
I do want my older brother's smile as a hand-me-down
I want so much flow, that one day a river cries me
I want criminal charges filed against the man who kidnapped my
    mother's laugh
I want Kayla from kindergarten to give me second chance just so I
    can break her
heart by the swing set like she did mine
I want chips to be 50 cents again
I wanna see a black name on the internet
and assume it graduated college

before I assume it's been shot

I wanna see a black face in a headline

and assume it's found a cure to cancer before I assume it went missing

I wanna know why we allow officers to take lives,

but don't require they learn how to save them

I wanna know how a security guard can shoot a boy in the stomach,

and civilians start CPR before he does

I don't wanna praise when a black body gets shot and survives

I want outrage anytime a bullet trespasses black skin

I want jail time for every single case,

I want battery to be charged so often,

the cop has to be 100% before unplugging the gun from his holster

I want these murderers hands so weak

they can't carry a tune, much less an automatic weapon

matter of fact, you can keep your indictment

I want the boy back

I want us to both die of natural causes

I want Trayvon to return home from the corner store whistling

I want a life

I wanna live

I wanna live

I wanna live

I wanna live in an all black neighborhood, on purpose

I wanna like it

I wanna look my family in the mirror at 75

Pull my grandchildren in from the cabinet corners of my reflection

I wanna gather them like crumbs around the stove

then sprinkle them with stories of my childhood,

I wanna let them marinate in the lives I've lived until they are
    seasoned enough
to pass on their own list of ingredients
I want black skin to do whatever it pleases, without any explanation
I want us to breathe, without permission.

LOAN FORGIVENESS

FOR BORROWED BREATH

When I say *fuck the police*
the middle finger is not an act of aggression
but a placeholder for all the words that go missing
when I say I'm pulled over and fear for my life
the fear is not that something may be stolen from me
it is the realization it was never mine to begin with.

KNEE REPLACEMENT

And so it was written
that black was no longer legally synonymous with death,
but still,
we blink just to believe ourselves whole again
eyes closed be the only way we wish our souls
on a heaven we wasn't painted into
how holy is it to know a god and his child,
that have chosen a color that is not yours
how half are we to question what's missing
how fraction was it to think we was equal divided
how hole must we be to forget the collective
how many knees does Kaep have to take to the chest,
before we take a stand
before we replace his bruises with a cape
before we make our own shield
the NFL not so different from a police union,
how quick they protect the pig's skin
replace this pledge with a plea
while the flag still wave
the field of the free
ain't no home for no slave.

GET OUT

AS TOLD FROM THE VOICE OF THE DEER ON THE WALL WHO SAW EVERYTHING

Sit, sink, replace, repeat.
a shell dressed as a person
walks into a mansion freely
then never walks anywhere else
sit sink replace repeat

it only takes two steps to cleanse a body of its black
everyone gets washed up in the sink
sit sink replace repeat
all colors fade to white
if you scrub hard enough
sit, sink, replace repeat
sit sink re-
oh but this boy's different,
sit sink replace repeat
Chris,
that's your name ain't it?
savior
you'd be Christ but your name is missing the cross,
you are not one to be crucified,

sit

sink

replace

repeat

oh my names not important,

I'm just a metaphor anyway

a hint of what darkness is behind and ahead of you,

I'm for shadowing,

sit

sink

replace

repeat

I've seen the boats of black bodies that went to battle before you

I don't blame them for sinking, either

especially when the ocean was anchored in so much racism

I've seen the way they embrace you

you me and that tea cup ain't so different you know

preserved on the outside to keep us empty inside

praised as long as we are possession

sit

sink

replace

repeat

all the hollows who sat in that chair before you was too proud to
    pick cotton,

too cotton mouth to quench their own thirst for freedom,

but here you are

all Nat Turner neck strength
all revolution mind-marching
all fed up and fist-clenching
sit
sink
replace
repeat
there's hope for you yet
sit
remember the clues I left you
sink
but return quickly to the surface
replace
your confusion with a way out
repeat
after me there were too many others here
let you be the last lest I be the last voice you hear
they believe you a beast anyway
it makes sense for their downfall
be you living up to the stereotype,
they tried to get you out, didn't know
what they got themselves into,
it started with a bid,
they put money on our heads
only right he die by the skull of a buck
pierced by the animal he hates most
and the thing he would rather be dead
a tragic love story ending where it started

the murder was a term of endearment

let it all burn in the background

let the ground deal with the funeral

let the scorched earth handle the arrangements

the fire will bury them just fine

you have to go now Chris!

I understand, it was too late for me

I only ask that you consider

there are others like you

that don't get the picture

waiting for a flash from a friend

for the strength to fight back

my name's not important Chris

I'm just a metaphor anyway

sit

sink

replace

repeat

sit, sink.

18 PASSENGER VAN

Without community, there is no liberation

AUDRE LORDE

Pass the right person the aux
Watch the car ride flip to an orchestra
Tiara is front row in the backseat
under-studying the DJ's every move
overstepping boundaries nobody knew they had
an opinion you didn't ask for
now strangely can't do without,
providing the origin story for every note the singer missed
a blueprint of how the song would have looked
if the vocal cords had more experience in architecture,
rewinds by request in case you miss a byte
notorious in how big she make a beat look
Naj tappin' the gas and brake to make the car do the 2-step
all the passengers dance along, by force
she's lost, and no one minds because it's a search *party*
GPS a click away, but we'd rather lose direction
than to know how far off course we've gone
text messages alert us that we're hours late to a gathering we planned,
our actions suggest we arrived soon as the car pulled up,
soon as everyone got dressed.
soon as we decided living was all the excuse we needed tonight
soon as we got together the get together started

Krystal's clear that she's not drinking dark
or anything else
again
for the last time
breath pregnant with last night's concoction
swears a child of bedside Baptist mustn't behave this way
"Right hand to ATL, I'm done drinkin'"
the words stutter-step out her mouth
suggest the next move
watch her fall back, or spring into action
Shaina's shell so strong she built a home in it
only invites a few inside to see the new place
can't believe how soft we all are after a few shots
how hard it is to cushion a friend
find a couch of people you can sink into
ability to see the best in people, even when there's none left,
scrape through the wreckage of a mangled relationship
pull out a dying pulse and build a companion from it,
Tiran knows the history of every fossil after a first impression
knows exactly how many bones a lover has collected
advises the whole car which digs are worth what
uses the dirt under his fingers to speak to the soil he's seen
will quickly tell all how he grew up-rooted
for him, a photo-op is synthesis
an excuse to be artificial
always changing
so much that he actually never does
Ami is never late to the party

is in fact a whole celebration in herself
smile a stack of confetti thrown to a blaze
laugh erupt so loud
the next town over turn to stone
presence such a gift
she sit right next to you
from a whole continent away
we enter, equal parts late and fashionable

Razjeá wrote the rules for the night
broke them all in order before guests arrived
Deshon in the corner battling against his own shadow
somehow they're both losing
AJ, Steve, & Mercedes somewhere in a back room
planning world domination
frame it as a family dinner for investors
secretly just an excuse to kick it
Darion in the center of the dance floor
trying to convince a Caribbean girl
his hips are where she come from
and it's about time she return home
puffs a flight to unpack the bags under his eyes
sketches a jug to prototype a new drink
Keith bought the supplies in cash
is shuttling almost inanimate people to safety
offers his basement as somewhere to crash
to prevent other collisions
does not agree with the party

but would rather us live this lifestyle

than have to style himself for our funeral(s)

Reggie lives next door

never calls the cops

nor complains of the noise

knows no matter where our actions land

our hearts are in the right place

promises to teach us a few things

if we stop moving long enough to listen

Daryl is a blur bouncing from one ear to the next

balancing a shot glass in one hand

and the absence where his heart used to be in the other

telling the story of a vampire to all who'll listen

"Love sucks, The End"

*Points to bite marks

*Curses the coffin for not loving him back

Jenna met up with us all earlier

before the night started making decisions for us

detailed how different we were

how the same we exist

agrees to take up space with us

cuz we all aliens

all stars in a game we never win

must keep playing anyway

Jeff doesn't exist as far as this paper is concerned

—Off the record—

made the party possible

played the role of the "cop knocking on door"

the scarecrow that keeps the vultures from
picking a black function bone dry
D'Real is the mayor of this town
elected us all his official cabinet
we never close, arms lazy susan
open whichever way he needs
Gabe got engaged last month and hasn't seen himself since
census goes out and his fiancé' forges his signature
misspells his middle name and loses her privilege of his last
bachelor party is now full of wing men
all chirping that he's so fly he can have any sky he desires
bar tender clouds his judgment further
shot glasses precipitating between words
a grammatical error is made
grandfather inside him creeps out
he wakes up next to someone who is not his type
but was bold, enough
exactly what the sentence was missing, this time
a single red cup gulps the last life from a bottle
no one can even remember opening
we toast one last time
funnel into whatever car can contain us,
head home, somehow feeling like we never left
elbow to elbow plastered between back seat and windshield
we realize, even if an indictment never comes
even if nothing is offered in consolation for how we're robbed
we've had all we needed right here
in the space between each other

in our willingness to go the distance
in our conviction to tell each other the truth
no matter how much it burns
or how hard it is to swallow.
we agreed that we're all up to it,
until the next time we get down to it.

ACKNOWLEDGMENTS

Thanks first be to God.

Thank you to Mrs. Croft, the 4th grade teacher who introduced me to poetry, then introduced my poetry to my mother.

Thanks to my immediate family: Brandon, Demetrius, Bobbi, Tabitha, and Chloe.

Thank you to the people that made the people that made me: Mary, Mike, Robert, Barbara.

Thanks to my Auntie Jasmine for being a best friend and writing partner when I needed both.

Thanks to Alchemy, Inc. for the circles and providing enough space to go around.

To the inner voices that said this was written too soon, and the outer ones who say it was long overdue.

To every poet who came before or after me in the Poetry Society at Eastern Michigan University.

To people that have faced down loaded military weapons and linked arms with me across state lines, Krystal, Shaina, Daryl, Jenna, Noelle, D'Real, Najwa, RAW, AA2F, Sydnee, Jackie, Shirley, Sasha, JC, Gloria, Durrell, Anthony, Zandra, and the brothers from MESA.

To the people who helped me understand my blackness; Sekou, My Brother My Sister, Malcolm Burton, my mother.

Thanks to the black creatives that inspire me to be a better artist, activist, and person through their craft; Tef Poe, Bria Erby, Damien McClendon, Ephraim Nehemiah, Alexx JL, Rudy Francisco, Danez Smith, Musics Einstein, Asaka the Renegade, Tyeal, Tristin Taylor, Asia Bryant-Wilkerson, Kitwana Clark, Derick Jerome, Deaira, Derek Dandridge, Jasmine Mans, DeAnn, Savon Bartley, Wavy Hardaway, Full Moon, and so many more.

For making the creation and storage of these poems possible huge thanks to Golden Bridge, Melissa Michaels, and Brooke Jordan.

DARIUS SIMPSON

is an award-winning spoken word artist and community organizer born in Akron, Ohio. He received his Bachelor Degree in Political Science from Eastern Michigan University, and uses poetry as a tool with which to heal, inform, and challenge his audience in their awareness of social, political, and economic oppression. Darius is featured as a protagonist in the film *Finding the Gold Within*, a documentary by Karina Epperlein on what it means to be a young black male in America. Simpon's work has also been featured in online publications such as Huffington Post, Mic, and Worldstar Hip Hop.

www.dariussimpsonspeaks.com

Made in the USA
San Bernardino, CA
26 April 2018